The Modern Monomyth

Mythological Storytelling

Book 1: Stages Of The Hero's Journey

Author: Joshua Coker

Editor: Julie Tarman

Copyright

Table of Contents

The Problem With Most Stories

As a fiction writer, the goal is to create a story that resonates with the audience. We all want to write something gripping that people will share with friends and family; a narrative that resonates with the reader, and keeps them revisiting the book for years to come. Unfortunately, this is easier said than done. Many of us start out with a passion for storytelling. We love exploring new worlds and developing complex characters. So we begin to write. But at some point, every storyteller realizes that in order to become a professional, we must hone our natural talent into a skill. So, what do we do? We buy books on writing. There's a book out there for everything. Some teach plot, others character. There are books that explain how to write action, suspense, conflict, dialogue, setting, theme, etc... But no matter how logical we structure our story, or how perfectly we construct our prose, the story doesn't seem to have that "X-factor" everyone wants in a story.

Even well known professionals face this problem. Think about how many times you've picked up a book by a writer you follow, or watched the latest installment in a franchise you love, only to be completely let down. How many forgettable novels or films have you come across in your lifetime? Some written by reputable authors and screenwriters. Even though the action, mystery, or romance was great, the story fell flat. The narrative lacked some mystical element that every great story seems to inherently possess.

This is the major problem every author, writer, poet, screenwriter, and storyteller face.

For years, I too struggled to find answers.

I looked.

But found none.

I read book after book in search of "the secret sauce." And while various aspects of my writing improved, I still hadn't found that aethereal magic. I wanted to know what made some stories rise to blockbuster status, while others did not. The same questions continued to plague my mind. Why do some sequels fail to capture the power of the first book in a series, even when written by the same author? Why do some movies with big-name movie stars, special effects, and huge budgets fail to do better than others with no-name actors, simple effects, and no budgets? After years of reading book after book, following every clue, and picking up bread crumb after bread crumb, I came across the Monomyth.

And finally everything clicked.

It felt as though the veil had been lifted from my eyes, and I could finally see the light. There were distinct elements that, when used correctly, imbued a story with seemingly mystical powers.

The power of myth.

Luckily you've stumbled upon this book, which means you don't have to spend years of study and research as I did. Within these pages, you'll learn the basic mythic structure. The purpose of this book is to serve as an introduction to the Monomyth, which means we will discuss everything at a high level. You won't have to worry about overly academic language or in depth psychological analysis. This book is written by a writer, for a writer. First I'll explain the definition of the Monomyth and it's early origins.

Then I'll teach you about the three act structure. I'll show you the differences between the known world and the special world of your story. You'll learn what really makes a character heroic. I'll teach you how plot and character feed off of each other, creating both an inner and outer journey. We'll outline the 18 distinct stages of the Hero's Journey and briefly discuss the main archetypes of the Monomyth. For each stage, this book provides at least four modern examples from well known stories. Each example will help you understand Hero's Journey, and help you identify the stages in your own book. Every chapter concludes with action steps, which you can immediately take on your story. These will help you infuse mythic power and life into the narrative. By the end of the book, you'll have a basic understanding of the Hero's Journey and a road map for your own story.

Ultimately, you'll ensure that your story to reaches it's full potential by taking full advantage of the Monomyth's ancient storytelling secrets.

So if that sounds like something that you're interested in, keep reading on!

Who will benefit from this book?

This book is geared specifically for storytellers, which means it can apply to just about anyone. However, it will probably be most appropriate for fiction authors. As mentioned above, this is the perfect tool to use through the entire story process. This can help you brainstorm ideas, outline your story, develop your characters, diagnose your narrative for plot holes, and analyze potential opportunities.

What if I'm a writer just starting out?

Then you are in luck!

I've been writing for nearly two decades now and I've read hundreds (literally) of writing books. Most of them touch on specific "craft" related items like structure, prose, dialogue, setting, blah, blah, blah... And after reading all of them, I was still left wondering how they all came together to form a compelling story. More importantly, I wanted to know why some stories resonated with me years after finishing them, while others were forgotten within days.

Like ingredients to a pizza, I knew I had to combine them all in order to make something. But I had no idea where, when, or how to do it. This is the book I wish I had back then. Learning the Monomyth is like having your grandma walk you through the steps of her secret recipe. You'll finally know how everything works together to create a true piece of art.

What if I already know the Monomyth?

For those of you that already have a solid understanding of the Monomyth--maybe you've already read *A Hero With A Thousand Faces*, or *The Writer's Journey*, or maybe just looked it up on the internet--this book will help in several ways. First off, it will reinforce what you already know. Second, this will give you a modern lens through which to view the storytelling process. Just as humankind evolves, so too does the Monomyth. Much of what Joseph Campbell gave us was based on ancient mythologies and fairy tales from around the world. The information and examples given in this book show how the Hero's Journey is being utilized today by modern storytellers. While this book only touches on foundational understanding, I still address a few major differences from the "historical" Monomyth. In future books, we'll delve even deeper into the new structure and archetypes of this modern age. Additionally, I list more than 72 specific examples from well-known stories that identify exactly where and why the Monomyth structure is used. Moreover, each section will have at least four distinct examples of how master storytellers have depicted each stage of the Monomyth. Lastly, I've included "action items" at the end of each chapter. These force you to think about your own story, and how you can ensure it reaches its full potential.

Now, with all of that out of the way, let's get down to the nitty gritty!

Common Misconceptions

Before we discuss the various stages of the Monomyth, it's important to understand a few common misconceptions writers have regarding the Hero's Journey. While the Monomyth has applications that span far beyond the scope of writing, its primary purpose is for storytelling. Generally speaking, there are two types of writers: "plotters" and "pantsers." Plotters are planners. They like to plan out everything in the story. World building, character studies, childhood histories, future books, etc... You name it, they plan it. Pantsers on the other hand, prefer to let the muse guide them through the story. They'll take a blank sheet of paper and idea, and write the day away. The truth is, all of us have a little bit of a plotter and a pantser inside. Each paradigm has strengths and each has weaknesses, but the best stories appear to come from writers who blend the two mindsets.

The Monomyth can accommodate the strengths of both writing types, and help each overcome their weaknesses. However, both plotters and pantsers hold a common misconception of what the Monomyth is, and how it should be used. Most of the confusion comes from the misnomer that the Monomyth is a template.

"Plotters"

Plotters see the Monomyth as a template and they rejoice. For their logical minds, the Hero's

Journey gives them a blueprint for the story. While there's nothing wrong with structuring a narrative, the problem arises when the story becomes a generic retelling of other stories. Every scene is cliche. Every character is one dimensional. In short, it's boring.

To illustrate this concept, we'll use architecture as an example. Every building requires a blueprint. The architect drafts one up, and gives it to the construction team. They use this document as an instruction manual. These directions explain where and how to configure each room. Windows, doors, a foundation, a roof, bathrooms, walls, etc. They all have to be placed precisely according to the blueprint. For this reason, the cheapest places to live are apartments. They are easy to build and cheap to make because they are all replicas of the same blueprint. They all look the same. The entryway is in the same place as the next door neighbor. The bathroom, the kitchen, and the living room are all located in the same place, made from the same materials. While these may be easy to make and reproduce, people do not pay much to live in them.

If you ask a friend--or yourself for that matter--what their dream home looks like, it's unlikely they would describe an apartment. When it comes to real estate, no one dreams of living in a generic place. Stories are the same. They are the real estate of the mind. No one is dying to spend money and time living in a world that is generic and boring.

Rather, they want something unique.

Inspiring.

Something worth their time, money, and energy.

Something they can talk about with all of their friends.

Let's consider mansions for a moment. The process to build them is nearly identical to that of an apartment. An architect drafts a blueprint and then construction begins. Essentially all of the same tools and materials are used to build. The timeframe for completion is roughly the same as well.

And yet, at the end of the day, the mansion sells for millions of dollars, whereas the apartment only rents for a few hundred.

So if the process is the same, what's the difference between the two buildings?

The mansion is unique.

It's different.

It's one of a kind.

It has an "X" factor.

It provides people an experience they would never find anywhere else.

This means that each time a new mansion is built, the architect must re-imagine the design. The architect is required to go back to the drawing board every time. They are forced to use their creative muscles over and over again. Each project has its own theme. Its own life. And yes, building such a structure requires hard work. Each section must fit together like a puzzle piece, or else the whole building falls apart.

But it's worth it.

Mansions are not easy to create, but everyone dreams of having one.

Masterpieces are the same way.

Unfortunately, many plotters take the "apartment complex" approach, using a paint-by-numbers scheme, rather than using their imagination.

Narratives written with this mindset suffer the same outcome as the apartments. Nobody pays money for them.

The Monomyth isn't a blueprint that tells you what to write and where to write it. It's more of a guide. Just as houses have key features such as doors, windows, kitchens, and roofs, stories have similar elements that are critical to the narrative.

"Pantsers"

Pantsers also assume the Monomyth is a template and avoid it like the plague. Nobody wants to be labeled as a "formulaic writer," especially a pantser. Their creative minds revolt against the very notion. And sure, at first glance, an author might give credence to this theory, as the Hero's Journey does follow a pre-designated format. However, upon further investigation, you will discover that this template serves more as a standard of storytelling rather than a paint-by-numbers instruction booklet.

In order to illustrate this point, let's use the automobile industry as an example. Most vehicles have tires, wheels, engines, seats, and doors. The same could be said of stories. Each is comprised of words, theme, plot, character, conflict, etc. But when we look at vehicles, there are several different types: cars, trucks, vans, SUVs, and more. Each one has a specific configuration based on its purpose. Those purposes are geared toward a particular individual's needs or desires. In fiction, genres serve a similar purpose. Science fiction, fantasy, romance, horror, thrillers, and on and on. Each one is a variation of narrative, specifically configured for a certain type of individual to obtain a particular response. Furthermore, there are different makes and models of vehicles that change and evolve over the years. This is also true of stories. Over the last few decades science fiction has evolved into various sub genres such as superhero fiction, steampunk, cyberpunk, and space opera, to name a few. And yet, whether or not it's a car, a truck, or a novel, in order for a product to sell in any industry, it must meet or exceed a specific standard. Not surprisingly, this is called the industry standard, and it is the basic requirements a consumer expects in order to purchase the product.

Most vehicles have at least four wheels, two windows, two doors, an engine, two seats, a trunk...

I think you get the point.

So while there may be thousands of different makes and models, vehicle standards run off of preset guidelines that are simple to understand and well-known by all. This standard is always evolving and changing to meet the needs and technology of mankind. The same holds true of stories. While there may be an infinite number of variations, every narrative follows an unspoken standard that consists of simple principles and guidelines well understood by all.

If you're still not sold, consider the opposite to be true. If automobile makers didn't have to follow a set standard, then what would prevent them from building cars without windows, or seats, or locks, or seatbelts?

The answer, *nothing*.

But then, "Who would buy these unsafe vehicles?" you might ask.

The answer, *no one*.

Which is exactly the point.

The reason why the mythic structure is so important to storytelling is because it serves as a standard for storytelling. There are millions of books, novels, and short stories that sit on shelves for years with no one reading them.

Why?

Because they didn't follow the standard, so nobody wants to read them.

Would you buy a house if it was missing a roof? No?

What if the architect told you he didn't want to follow a template because it's too formulaic? What if he told you he preferred to let the building grow from his imagination? Would that make you feel any better? Would that convince you to buy the house? No?

And yet this is what thousands of would-be writers do every day.

Just as certain physics dictate the movements of celestial bodies, so too does an invisible force guide story structure. That force, is the Monomyth.

As you will see throughout examples in this book, the Monomyth allows for infinite possibilities when telling a story.

How to use the Monomyth when writing

As mentioned above, many creatives claim that templates are too "restrictive." They complain that a preset format prevents them from tapping into the full potential of their imagination. They will tell you that sticking to a pre-designated route constricts narrative possibilities. These are the same writers that would prefer to go "off-roading" with their story. They would rather explore the unknown wilderness of their imaginations, in hopes of capturing some exotic, ethereal feeling.

But the truth is, writing is like driving. Without proper navigation, you can get lost or stuck. And that is exactly where many writers find themselves after days, weeks, months, and even years of creative "trailblazing."

Lost and stuck.

If you intended to take a trip across country, would you just get in the car one day and drive aimlessly with no plan? Or would you sit down and map out your journey? Would you decide which roads where most appropriate, or would you wait until you hit a dead end before changing course? Would you plan rest stops and lodging for the night, or would you just drive until you fall asleep at the wheel?

I think most would agree that planning out a trip is the most effective way to ensure you get to your destination. But when it comes to storytelling, most writers set out with no destination in mind. They aspire to take a journey that spans across time and space, but they have no game plan to get from point A to point B. And the sad part is that they expect the reader to pay gas money along the way.

If you were the reader, would you want to foot the bill for a trip like that?

I think not.

The Monomyth is like a road map. It can help you plan the most effective story, so that both you and the audience can enjoy the trip. For those of you who may have gotten lost in the fields of imagination, it can help get your story back on track. The mythic structure will ensure your story has a clear destination and purpose.

In order to illustrate this common theme, I've selected four modern examples (Lord of the Rings, Star Wars, Harry Potter, and Hunger Games). Each is widely known, commercially successful, and follows the Hero's Journey to the T. However, each one is wildly different from the others in genre, setting, theme, character, and plot, thus demonstrating the Monomyth's flexibility and versatility.

Introduction to the Monomyth

What do Star Wars, Lord of the Rings, Harry Potter, and Hunger Games all have in common? Yes, they're all Hollywood blockbusters. Yes, they all have great special effects. Yes, they all made hundreds of millions of dollars. However, when we look at the narrative, the main aspect that each has in common is that they all follow the Monomyth format.

What is the Monomyth?

Well I'm glad you asked, because this book will serve as an overview of the Monomyth. First, we'll discuss meanings and origins of the Monomyth. Second, we'll look at the basic components of the Monomyth. And third, we'll discuss why the Monomyth is important for everyday life.

What is the Monomyth?

The definition of the word Monomyth comes from two Greek root words; mono, meaning "one," and mythos, meaning "story." So when you combine the two, you get the "one story." The connotation is that there is one underlying structure to all stories. In recent years, the term has become synonymous with the "Hero's Journey." Additionally, it has loose connections with the "Fool's Journey," which is used in Tarot.

Furthermore, the Monomyth seems to be as old as humanity itself. Aspects of the Monomyth can be seen in stories throughout human history. Although several academics studied this idea throughout the ages, it wasn't really popularized until 1949, when Professor Joseph Campbell published the book, *The Hero With A Thousand Faces*. Campbell worked as a comparative mythologist and spent his life studying ancient stories and fairy tales from around the world. His research revealed that these stories and fairy tales shared common elements. It was as if each ancient story followed the same story format. He named it the Monomyth after a novel by James Joyce, however he also referred to it as the Hero's Journey. Furthermore, using the work of Sigmund Freud and Carl Jung, Professor Campbell showed that every stage in the process had connections with human psychology. Since then, numerous books have been written on the subject. Moreover, several stories, movies, and even video games were written following the Monomyth template. Hence, the earlier reference to Star Wars, Lord of the Rings, Harry Potter, and Hunger Games.

Over the last few decades, the Monomyth has evolved to incorporate modern day storytelling techniques. This book is the first in a series of books designed to teach the modern day Monomyth. Particularly, this will serve as an introduction to the stages in the Hero's Journey and how they have evolved into modern times. It will touch on basic concepts and foundational knowledge. Future books will take an in-depth look at each stage, step and archetype in the narrative structure, and discuss how they can be used for contemporary stories.

The following video explains the best reference materials for the Monomyth, if you wish to explore the subject even further.

How is the Hero's Journey Structured?

On a basic level, the Hero's Journey is broken into a three act structure. Within those acts, Joseph Campbell identified 17 specific stages. However, others, such as screenwriter Christopher Vogler, author of *The Writer's Journey*, partition them even further into steps. Since this is a basic overview, we will only look at the stages. However, for the sake of modernization, one additional stage has been included in this book.

Three Main Acts

The three main acts are:
1. Separation
2. Initiation
3. Return

In the first act of Separation, the hero must leave his normal world behind by accepting the call to adventure, meeting helpers/mentors, and crossing the threshold into the special world. During the second act of Initiation, the hero must face the road of trials, approach the innermost cave, face death, and receive the ultimate boon. In the last act of the Return, the hero must go back to the normal world to share the boon with society. Normally this culminates in a final climax or battle, where the hero uses all that he's learned along the journey to win the day.

18 Stages

There are 18 distinct stages in the modern day Monomyth. Joseph Campbell identified 17, and this book has added one for modernization purposes. They are listed below:

1. Ordinary World (This stage was added for modernization)
2. Call To Adventure
3. Refusal Of Call
4. Supernatural Aid
5. Crossing The Threshold
6. Belly Of The Whale
7. The Road Of Trials
8. Meeting With The Goddess
9. Woman as Temptress
10. Atonement With The Father
11. Apotheosis
12. Retrieve The Ultimate Boon
13. Refusal Of The Return
14. The Magic Flight

15. Rescue from Without
16. The Crossing Of The Return Threshold
17. Master Of Both Worlds
18. Freedom To Live

Archetypes

Aside from the three main plot events and 18 stages, the Monomyth is also comprised of several archetypes. These are characters that fulfill major roles in the story and represent a psychological maturation that all humans go through during life. The hero, mentor, and villain are just a few of the basic archetypes that comprise the Monomyth. As an example, Gandalf, Obi Wan, and Dumbledore are the epitome of the mentor archetype. While archetypes are critical to the Monomyth, they do not fit the scope of this book. If you wish to learn more about archetypes, please refer to my other books, courses and videos on the subject.

Why is the Monomyth important?

First off, it helps writers write. On the surface level, the Monomyth is a great tool for storytellers. It is a great template to structure anything from a screenplay to a novel. It also provides authors a road map for their narrative. If you feel your story has gone off of the beaten path, this outline will guide you back to the road.

Moreover, the Monomyth gives us insight into our own lives. On a deeper level, the Monomyth helps us evaluate our own lives. Whether you're writing a novel, going out on a date, or giving a job interview, we all tell stories everyday. What many people don't realize is that each of us are living a story, our own little soap opera if you will. The story of your life is told through recurring events and actions that push you toward maturation. For example, when a young man or woman accepts the call to adventure and joins the military, they leave their normal world. They are confronted with new obstacles and challenges in the proceeding years. And at some point, they leave the military and return back to society changed forever by their experiences. Moreover, these veterans--or modern day heroes--bring the lessons they learned in the field back to the normal world. This revitalizes society on many different levels. Family, business, and technology are just a few of the areas that benefit from these heroic acts. The same thing happens to students who attend a college. Or a couple who become parents. On a personal level, the Monomyth provides us a vehicle to analyze our own narrative, and to help us understand our failures and successes in a meaningful way.

Recap

1. Monomyth means the "one story."
2. Elements of the Monomyth can be found in nearly all forms of mythology and fairy tales from around the world.
3. It's comprised of a three act structure, and has several recurring archetypes.
4. The basic uses are for writing and story structure.
5. Many people find it as a helpful tool in understanding their own life's story.

As I mentioned before, this is just to cover the the basics of the Monomyth. Over the course of this book, I intend to provide several explanations on the different aspects of the Hero's Journey, and analyze more advanced Stages in the narrative structure.

If you'd like to hear more about the Monomyth and Hero's Journey, feel free to watch my YouTube video about it here[1].

---

[1] https://www.youtube.com/watch?v=rezosnHkwK8&t=133s

What Makes a Hero?

Before we can go any further we must clear something up...

What exactly is a hero?

I mean, since the Monomyth is also known as the Hero's Journey, shouldn't we know who the heck the hero is?

In a word, yes.

But how do I know which character is my hero?

Some might say that a hero is the protagonist. That is, the driving force of the story. Others may say that a hero is the main character. This means that the story is told primarily through their viewpoint. While they're both partially true, according to the Monomyth, a hero is something more.

In order for someone to qualify as a hero, they must leave the normal world in search of the boon. They venture out into the special world where they face trials and tribulations. After many tests they achieve the boon, and return it back to the normal world. And that is the major difference between protagonists, main characters, and heroes in the Monomyth structure. The hero must return the boon back to the normal world. Meaning that the hero doesn't just save himself, or his friends. He doesn't just retrieve the boon and keep the power for himself. The hero returns to the community and helps restore society. He shares the power of the boon. In ancient times, boys would be plucked from their mother's tents and taken to the warriors. They were taught to fight, and hunt. Then they would go out into the wilderness with the other hunters to find food. The hero's mission was only complete once he brought food back. At that point he revitalized the tribe, by providing food for the winter months. Similar parallels can be seen in today's society when young men and women enlist in the military to become soldiers.

Given the fact that the hero goes from the known world to the unknown world, they must learn new lessons, and ultimately change their way of thinking. Normally this requires your hero to have a character arc. Meaning, they will change over the course of the narrative. For example, in a story where the hero was a lonely orphan with no self confidence, the journey would force them to become a strong confident leader. Consider Luke Skywalker, Harry Potter, Frodo Baggins, Bilbo Baggins, or Katniss Everdeen. Each goes through a similar rebirth. Each character follows the Hero's Journey.

So, while a hero can serve as a protagonist, or a main character (or both), not all protagonists and main characters are necessarily heroes.

Separation: The First Act of the Hero's Journey

As I mentioned previously, we will dissect each act of the Hero's Journey. We will break it down into core components, which are the stages. In this chapter, we'll discuss the Separation Act of the Monomyth. Remember, the Hero's Journey is broken up into three main acts: Separation (also known as departure), Initiation (also know as trials/tests), and the Return.

Purpose of the Separation Act

In many ways, the Separation Act is the most important. Not only do audiences decide whether or not they want to participate in the story based on this portion, but it has several duties. First this act sets the tone, genre, and theme of the story. Second, it raises the dramatic question. For example, in Lord of the Rings, the dramatic question revolves around whether or not Frodo and the fellowship will successfully destroy the one ring and defeat Sauron. Another job of this act is to introduce key characters, particularly the hero. Several contemporary stories also introduce the main antagonist during this act. Most importantly, the audience needs to know about their flaws, quirks, needs, and desires. Is your hero an ex marine that struggles with an alcohol problem? Or a staunch business woman that will do anything for a promotion? In Star Wars we meet Luke Skywalker, an orphaned farm boy who lives with his aunt and uncle, but secretly wishes to join the rebellion. Lastly, this section introduces the audience to world mechanics, rules, and technology. Is there magic? Can people teleport? Do people only travel by horse and buggy? What currency do they use? In the first scene of Harry Potter we learn there are anamorphic witches, magical wizards, and flying motorcycles. In the first act of Hunger Games we learn that Panem is a post apocalyptic world. While those who live near the Capitol enjoy access to futuristic technology and accommodations, most citizens live in poverty and destitution.

Separation Stages

In order to achieve all of the above goals, the storyteller must make use of the six stages in the Separation Act. Below is a list for easy reference:

1. Ordinary World (This stage was added for modernization)
2. Call to Adventure
3. Refusal of Call
4. Supernatural Aid
5. Crossing the Threshold
6. Belly of the Whale

In the following chapters we'll analyze these stages in more detail.

Stage One: Ordinary World (also known as the Mundane World)

In this stage, the storyteller's job is to show the hero in their natural habitat, going through their daily rituals. If done correctly, this will also introduce us to the world the hero lives in, rules he abides by, physics that govern them, and technology they use. Most heroes start out fairly ordinary in strengths and skills. The aspect that makes the audience care about the hero revolves around their flaws. Quirks, scars, and physical limitations are all outer expressions of an inner flaw. Show us a woman that struggles with an alcohol addiction, or a man that can't tell the truth to the people he loves, and suddenly we're hooked. Why? Because they face the same demons we face in real life. That and the flaws you present in the beginning lay the groundwork for the character arc, and ultimately the hero's victory in the end.

Lord of the Rings

Frodo Baggins is an orphan who lives with his Uncle Bilbo. Hobbits come from a farm-like village called Hobbiton, which is located far away from the great kingdoms of Middle-earth. When we first meet Frodo, he is reading a book and waiting for the wizard Gandalf the Grey. We learn quickly that Frodo is a kind, inquisitive halfling that enjoys spending time with his friends Sam, Merry, and Pippin.

Star Wars:

Luke Skywalker is an orphan that works as a moisture farmer for his Uncle Owen. They live on a desert planet called Tatooine, in the backwater section of the galaxy. Luke secretly wishes to join the Rebellion and become a fighter pilot like his friend Biggs. When we first meet Luke, he is cleaning off droids that his uncle recently purchased. They mention their involvement with the Rebellion and Luke stumbles on a hidden message. He wonders if the droids may actually be property of Old Ben Kenobi, a "crazy old wizard" that lives nearby.

Harry Potter:

   Harry Potter is an orphan that lives under the stairs in his Uncle and Aunt's house. His foster parents have lied to him his whole life in an attempt to prevent him from becoming a wizard. Harry is an inquisitive boy that wonders if there's more to life. Around his birthday, strange events begin to occur. He can seemingly talk to snakes and do magical feats. Owls flood the doors with mail for him. Eventually a giant bearded wizard named Hagrid breaks him free of the prison his Uncle and Aunt have created for him.

Hunger Games:

   Katniss Everdeen is a gifted hunter and archer. When we first meet her she is illegally hunting in the woods of District 12 on the day of the reaping. She and her best friend Gale imagine what it would be like to run away into the woods, so that they can escape the Hunger Games. Only one tribute from District 12 has ever survived the games, and he is known around the town as a crazy drunken fool. Unfortunately, both of them must return to the city square to take part in the lottery.

Stage Two: Call to Adventure (Enticing Incident)

In this stage the storyteller must give the hero an initial mission. This normally is conveyed through a herald who approaches the hero and tells them to go on a journey. Other times a hero is forced into a situation that is beyond their control. While this task may seem insignificant at the time, it will force the hero to come in contact with the mentor and eventually commit him to the overall journey.

Lord of the Rings:

After placing it in the fire, Gandalf realizes that the ring Bilbo left behind is the One Ring of Power created by Sauron in the fires of Mount Doom. Knowing he cannot take the ring himself, the wizard asks Frodo to care for the Ring. He instructs Frodo to take it out of the Shire and meet him at the Prancing Pony. Meanwhile, Gandalf leaves to consult with Saruman, the head of his order.

Star Wars:

After saving Luke from Sand People, Obi Wan takes the hero back to his hut. Then he gives Luke his father's lightsaber. Obi Wan tells Luke history about his father and the Jedi. He explains that Darth Vader was once his pupil and that Vader killed Luke's father. Once they discover the full message from Princess Leia, Obi Wan Kenobi tells Luke he must come with him to Alderaan and learn the ways of the force.

Harry Potter:

Harry receives multiple letters from owls requesting that he attend Hogwarts, a school for witchcraft and wizardry. His Uncle and Aunt move to a dungeon-like house on an island to prevent the wizards from finding Harry. Despite their best efforts, a giant bearded wizard named Hagrid breaks in and rescues Harry. He informs Harry that he is the son of two of the most powerful wizards in the world. He explains that Harry must go to Hogwarts and learn to become a wizard.

Hunger Games:

Katniss and all the other children of age are forced to attend The Reaping. This is an annual event where children are selected in a lottery to be tributes in the Hunger Games. After taking blood samples and names, Katniss and her sister Prim are herded off with the rest of the girls from District 12. Then when the Capitol representative, Effie, pulls the card from the bucket, she calls Prim's name out as the female tribute.

Stage Three: Refusal of Call

In this stage the storyteller's job is to show the hero refusing the call. This is a vital step in humanizing the hero. When faced with change, most people's initial reaction is to fight against it. Depicting this natural response will help readers empathise with the hero on a psychological level. Resistance to change is a character flaw that all people share. Showing this resistance will set up the character arc at the end of the story, when the hero is prepared to sacrifice himself for the cause. Once the hero refuses, they normally go through a period of boredom or setbacks, which "punish" the hero for their resistance to psychological change. Eventually the situation gets so bad that the hero either changes their mind, or is forced to go on the journey. Occasionally the refusal is depicted by another character. Quite often this "fill-in" character is an Uncle or Aunt who serves as caretaker for the hero. Generally this is when the hero is already willing to go on the adventure.

Lord of the Rings:

Frodo doesn't want anything to do with the ring of power and offers it back to Gandalf. Gandalf explains that he is too powerful to wield the ring and that it must be someone like Frodo, who is not tempted by its power, to carry it. After realizing the stakes, Frodo accepts Gandalf's call to adventure.

Star Wars:

Luke tells Obi Wan that he has to stay and help his Uncle Owen with the harvest. In reality, Luke is nervous and second guessing himself. He's not sure if he has what it takes to become a rebellion fighter. Later Luke discovers that stormtroopers killed his Uncle and Aunt. Full of rage, and renewed with purpose, he sets out to Mos Eisley with Obi Wan. He vows to go to Alderaan and become a Jedi, like his father.

Harry Potter:

Harry's uncle boards up the windows and eventually moves the family to a shack to avoid letters from the owls. Harry also hesitates when Hagrid comes, stating that he's just a normal boy. Hagrid informs him that he is a wizard, and uses magic to prove his claims. After that Harry follows his new mentor to Diagon Alley to begin his adventure into the world of witchcraft and wizardry.

Hunger Games:

No one in the district, including Katniss, wants to be picked for the Hunger Games because it means fighting to the death in an arena with other tributes. Her younger sister Primrose is selected from the raffle. Given Prim's age, it is unlikely she will survive against older tributes. In order to save her sister, Katniss volunteers in her stead. Because of this sacrificial act, Katniss must now face death in the gladiator-like arena of the Hunger Games.

Stage Four: Supernatural Aid

In this stage the hero accepts the call, either because they are forced to out of boredom, or necessity. Once they've accepted the call, a mentor will come into the story in order to help them along the way. In mythology, this individual normally had magical powers, so they were considered a supernatural aid. In modern myth this can still be the case, however we do see many mentors who act more like teachers. They are individuals who have been to the special world and can impart their wisdom on the hero. Sometimes the mentor acts as a herald, so they've already been introduced to the hero. Other times it seems that fate puts them in the path of the hero. Whatever the case, the mentor's job is to prepare the hero for the special world. They will provide tools and information that will assist the hero on the journey. In many cases the mentor also provides a psychological center for the hero to stay inwardly grounded when facing internal challenges.

Lord of the Rings:

After Gandalf explains that he cannot take the ring because it would wield a power too terrible to imagine, Frodo understands that the wizard needs help. He agrees to take the ring and bring it to the Prancing Pony in the town of Brea. From this point on, Gandalf acts as the supernatural aid to not just Frodo, but Aragorn and the rest of the heroes in The Fellowship. In the second story, Aragorn, Gimli, and Legolas go searching for Merry and Pippin. While tracking them they are lead into Fangorn Forest and they come across a white wizard who they believe to be Saruman. Later they discover it is Gandalf reborn. Gandalf the White continues to mentor the trio throughout the rest of the story.

Star Wars:

After discovering that the Empire killed his Aunt and Uncle, Luke accepts the call and accompanies Obi Wan to Mos Eisley. From this point on the old Jedi master trains Luke in the ways of the Force using the lightsaber his new mentor provided. In all three films Obi Wan serves as the supernatural aid and primary mentor. In the second movie Yoda also serves as a mentor. However, if you consider the original trilogy as one giant ongoing story, then Yoda's role is more accurately described as the goddess figure (or the divine). This will be discussed in a later stage.

Harry Potter:

After Hagrid sets Harry's uncle straight, Harry follows Hagrid to Diagon Alley to get all of the wizarding tools he needs. Hagrid acts as the first mentor to Harry. He teaches him the basics of wizards, helps him get money from the bank, and then he takes him to a few stores so he can buy an owl and a wand. After that, he escorts Harry to the bus station. The information and tools Hagrid gives Harry help him further down his journey. Later in the series several other wizards, including Dumbledore, act as Harry's mentors.

Hunger Games

After the Capitol custodian (and story herald), Effie, selects her sister, Katniss volunteers as tribute instead. She and Peeta are then taken on a train where they meet Haymitch. He is the only tribute from District 12 to ever win the Hunger Games. Although they do not get along at first, eventually Haymitch proves to be an extremely helpful mentor. The information and tools he provides are essential for the journey, and end up saving Katniss and Peeta multiple times.

Stage Five: Crossing Threshold

At this point in the journey, the hero finally sets out on the adventure. He will meet several threshold guardians. Each one will test the hero. Some will become friends or allies, while others will become rivals or enemies. The closer he gets to the threshold of adventure, the less familiar things are. By the time he crosses it, he is in a completely unknown or unexplored area, commonly referred to as the special world (also known as the unknown world, or the adventure world). This is a place that contrasts with the normal world where the hero started out. It has different rules and sometimes physics, which causes the hero to feel disoriented upon arrival.

Lord of the Rings:

Frodo, and the other Hobbits leave the shire. First they are chased by Farmer Maggot. Then they are stalked by the Nine Ringwraiths as they attempt to meet Gandalf at the Prancing Pony. Once they get to the bar they encounter several unsavory individuals, including Strider. He helps them evade the Nine Wraiths, then leads them deeper into the frontier where they learn to hunt, fight, camp, and hide.

Star Wars:

Once they have arrived in Mos Eisley, Luke and Obi Wan must evade stormtroopers. While in the Cantina, they meet Han and Chewbacca. Spies, crime bosses, criminals, and bounty hunters act as threshold guardians, trying to prevent them from leaving Tatooine. After they blast out of the spaceport, they must evade star destroyers, shoot down TIE fighters, and jump to lightspeed.

Harry Potter:

Harry tours Diagon Alley and the Bank learning more about this new world. Harry learns about goblins, wizards, and witches. He also learns that his parents died at the hands of Voldemort, an evil wizard that he apparently defeated when he was a baby. Not only does he receive his own owl, but he is tested in order to obtain his wand. Both he and Hagrid go on a minor side quest to the bank. While there, they must pass a few obstacles and threshold guardians to obtain a secret item for Professor Dumbledore.

Hunger Games:

Katniss is forced to quickly say goodbye to her mother, Prim, and Gale. Capitol guards take Katniss and Peeta aboard a train to the Capitol. There they meet Effie and Haymitch. Both initially serve as threshold guardians. Effie represents the ignorance and lavishness of the Capitol. Haymitch is a victor that wallows in a drunken stupor, trying to drown his demons in alcohol. In order to obtain their wisdom about the special world, Katniss must learn how to befriend both of them. Once they arrive in the Capitol, they are surrounded by strange citizens that dress and drink lavishly. They are cleaned and groomed by stylists. Katniss must learn to trust Cinna, her personal stylist, so that she may obtain the symbolic power of District 12, and ultimately the favor of sponsors.

Stage Six: Belly of the Whale

The belly of the whale marks the hero's first taste of death. First the hero is swallowed up by something and seemingly dies. Then the hero escapes or comes back to life. Sometimes the hero drowns, or is dismembered. This imagery is symbolic of a baptism into the special world. The hero enters and dies, then is reborn into the new world.

Lord of the Rings:

Frodo is hunted by the Nine Ringwraiths. He appears to die both at the inn near the Prancing Pony and when he is stabbed on the ruins of Weathertop. In both instances Strider saves Frodo and the other Hobbits. Arwen takes him to Elrond, who is able to save him from his mortal wound from the Morgul blade. From this point on Frodo is reborn. He is no longer just a Hobbit from Hobbiton. He is the hero who took the ring to Rivendell and survived a deathly blow. Shortly after, Frodo realizes he is the only person with the fortitude to serve as ringbearer.

Hunger Games:

For Katniss the belly of the whale is far more subtle. She enters the Capitol which represents the whale. This is particularly true during the Parade of Tributes, where she and Peeta are marched into a large arena and put on display for the world to see. As members of District 12, not many people are rooting for them. However, Cinna's fire outfit turns them into the talk of the town. Not only are they baptized into the Capitol culture, from this point on, Katniss has been "reborn" in the eyes of the citizens. Now she and Peeta are favored tributes. Winning this fandom becomes part of the overall strategy and eventually a key reason the two are spared at the end of the story.

Star Wars:

Luke and his friends are caught in the Death Star's tractor beam and "swallowed whole." Later they must submerge themselves in secret cargo bins, in order to hide from stormtroopers. Later they defeat a scanning party and take the stormtrooper armor. In this sense, Luke and his team survived certain death are now "reborn" in the imperial armor. Their disguise allows them to sneak past several threshold guardians and ultimately find the princess.

Harry Potter:

For Harry this stage takes place in the train to Hogwarts. First he must figure out how to get through Platform 9 ¾, which is his first deliberate magical act in this new world. Once on the other side, he has been baptized into the world of wizardry. Once on the train, he meets his two main companions, Hermione and Ron.

Recap

Just to recap, the separation act is where we meet the hero in their normal world and learn about their flaws, problems, and motives. We are introduced to their sidekicks, rivals, and mentors. The hero receives a call to adventure and shortly after, meets a mentor or guide who gives them tools and information for the journey ahead. As the hero sets out toward the special world, they face multiple threshold guardians that try to prevent them from crossing the threshold of adventure. Once they cross the threshold, they are normally swallowed up into the "belly of the whale," where they get their first taste of death, and are baptized into the special world. Throughout this act, the hero meets several characters, including sidekicks, heralds, mentors, threshold guardians, and antagonistic forces.

Action Items

Take a moment to write down the answers to these questions:

- FLAW: What is your hero's major flaw, weakness, or crutch? This should be a thought process or lie that prevents them from reaching their full potential.
    - ☐ Addiction
    - ☐ Greed
    - ☐ Lust
    - ☐ Reliance on rules, laws, system, logic
    - ☐ Overly dependent or independent
    - ☐ Requires validation, attention
    - ☐ Overconfidence
- SCAR: Why have they developed this flaw? What caused this mindset?
    - ☐ Abuse
    - ☐ Death of a loved one
    - ☐ Break up
    - ☐ Lost job
    - ☐ Promotion
    - ☐ Family responsibilities
    - ☐ Job responsibilities
    - ☐ Perceived obligation
- HERO INTRO: What's the most effective way to introduce the character?

- [ ] Working at their job
    - [ ] Farmer chasing down horses
    - [ ] Cop saving a child from a criminal
    - [ ] Business woman aggressively closing a deal
    - [ ] Pick up artist flirting with a girl
- [ ] Interacting with their friends/family
    - [ ] Airship captain interacting with her crew
    - [ ] Parent talking with their children
    - [ ] Dog barking at a cat
- [ ] Interacting with the environment
    - [ ] Hunter hunting deer
    - [ ] Magician using magic
    - [ ] Book worm reading a book
- WORLD PHYSICS: How can you best display the general world dynamics?
    - [ ] Spaceships flying by a planet
    - [ ] A giant war between humans, elves, and orcs
    - [ ] Magic wizards using magical powers

- ☐ Juxtapose poor townspeople next to high tech Capitol guards
- CATALYST: What is the initial incident that causes the hero to stray from their normal world and ultimately puts them in the path of the mentor? The catalyst can take form in several different scenarios. Perhaps the hero...
  - ☐ Helps someone in need
  - ☐ Fulfills a duty requirement
  - ☐ Looks into something out of curiosity
  - ☐ Goes chasing after something/someone
  - ☐ Searches for something they've lost
- REFUSAL: What causes your hero to initially refuse their mission?
  - ☐ Fear of change
  - ☐ Conflicting priorities
  - ☐ Believes the mission is beneath them
- ACCEPTANCE: What causes your hero to eventually accept the mission?
  - ☐ Duty
  - ☐ Boredom
  - ☐ Possibility of reward
  - ☐ No other choice

- ☐ Someone forces them
- MENTOR: Who is best suited to help your hero along his journey? Who has knowledge of the special world (also known as the unknown world, or the adventure world), that can bestow information upon the hero?
  - ☐ Old man or woman
  - ☐ Soldier
  - ☐ Child
  - ☐ Crazy person
  - ☐ Old friend
  - ☐ Business associate
- TALISMANS: What tools does the mentor provide the hero to help him on the journey?
  - ☐ Book
  - ☐ Sword
  - ☐ Motto
  - ☐ Gem
  - ☐ Necklace
  - ☐ Shield
  - ☐ Potion
  - ☐ Spell

- THRESHOLD GUARDIANS: While crossing the threshold, who are some people that can test the hero? Some may join the hero, while others will become his enemies.
    - ☐ Transporter (driver, pilot, boatman)
    - ☐ Bartender
    - ☐ Fighters
    - ☐ Lovers
    - ☐ Rivals
    - ☐ Colleagues
    - ☐ Antagonist's army/forces
    - ☐ Contagonist
- FIRST TASTE OF DEATH: How can you depict the hero having their first brush with death before fully entering the special world?
    - ☐ Captured/kidnapped
    - ☐ Swallowed up by large animal (like a whale)
    - ☐ Tractor beam
    - ☐ Antagonist/contagonist hurts/kills hero or someone they know
    - ☐ Nearly drown
    - ☐ Loss of lover/crush (if romance)

Initiation: The Second Act of the Hero's Journey

As you already know, the Hero's Journey is broken up into three main acts, 1) Separation, 2) Initiation, and 3) Return. In this section, we will discuss the "Initiation" act of the Monomyth. This is where the hero sets out into the special world. He faces obstacles and learns new lessons, which will help him defeat the antagonistic force. He will also encounter several new people along the way.

Purpose of the Initiation Act

In many ways, the Initiation Act is the most exciting. Not only is this where most of the action happens, but it serves as a testing ground for the hero and his allies. The purpose of the Initiation Act is to test the hero and their allies with multiple obstacles that gradually build in difficulty over time. It introduces more key characters such as the shapeshifter, trickster, and shadow. The hero will get their first glimpse of the special world, and its difficulties. The hero experiences death and sacrifice on a much deeper level than he did in the separation act. In the first half of the Initiation stage, the hero must face a series of tests that teach him valuable lessons about the special world. After these trials he will go through the transformative stages in order to find balance in his life. According to Joseph Campbell, ancient myths had four types of transformations: 1) meeting with the goddess, 2) atonement with the father, 3) apotheosis, and 4) the ultimate boon. In modern stories we normally see the hero go through all of these stages or a variation of them.

When the hero enters this act, they are normally running from the antagonistic force. In the middle, they come up with a plan to fight against it. By the end, they have faced the antagonistic force head on, and perhaps have won a momentary victory.

Initiation Stages

In order to achieve the above narrative goals, the storyteller must make use of the six stages in the Initiation Act. Below is a list for easy reference (continuing from the Separation Act):

7. The road of Trials

8. Meeting with the Goddess

9. Temptation

10. Atonement with the Father

11. Apotheosis

12. Retrieve the Ultimate Boon

In the following chapters we'll analyze these stages in more detail.

Stage 7: The Road of Trials

After leaving the belly of the whale, the hero will be completely immersed in the special world and fully on their journey. During the road of trials, the hero will be on the run from the antagonistic force. This will entail running, hiding, licking wounds, seeking shelter, and trying to catch their breath. Along the path, the hero will meet more threshold guardians like ogres, goblins, dragons, monsters, and dark nights. Many times the heroes must face difficult terrain along the road of trials. This could be quicksand, high cliffs, dark caves, crashing waves, asteroids, and several other obstacles. The point of these trials is to teach the hero the thematic lessons needed to complete the journey. The hero may have to face a sphinx or solve a riddle. This stage normally is the longest and most episodic of the story. Normally this includes at least three trials, although it may have as many tests as necessary to teach the hero the lesson needed.

Lord of the Rings:

In the Fellowship of the Ring, Frodo and Hobbits run from the Nine Ringwraiths. Later the fellowship tries the Gap of Rohan, but must change direction because of Saruman's spy-like crows. Later they nearly die on snowy cliffs. Lastly they must solve the dwarvish riddle in order to enter the Mines of Moria while facing the squid monster in the lake. In the latter two books/movies the heroes face other trials such as Uruk Hai, trolls, Nazgul, orcs, men of the east, evil wizards, elven guards, Gondor guards, and giant spiders. They travel through mazes, dead swamps, volcanic ash, and living woods.

Star Wars:

In *A New Hope*, Luke and his team hide from stormtroopers. They must figure out how to release their ship. Obi Wan leaves to shut down the tractor beam, while Luke and Han discover the princess' whereabouts. Then they break into the detention center and rescue Leia. In the following two films, they face snow monsters, giant machines, bounty hunters, swamp monsters, ogre-like pigs, spider droids, tribal bear-creatures, and bike chases.

Hunger Games:

During this stage, Katniss and the other tributes are tested and evaluated by the game makers and sponsors. Katniss meets the other tributes and shows her ability with the bow and arrow, while Peeta displays his skills with camouflage. They face similar challenges in the sequels, however many of Katniss' new tests revolve around making friends, political statements, and inspiring others.

Harry Potter:

In the first movie, Harry and his friends face ogres, spiders, Cerberus, unfriendly teachers, and rivals during his trial phase. They learn many spells and lessons that help them later in the story. Additionally, most of his tests happen in a school, but he also must go into a dark forest and the Quidditch arena. The latter stories continue with similar tests and trials, however as Harry gets older, he must also learn how to bring together a team of wizards to fight against Voldemort's forces.

Stage 8: Meet with the Goddess

In this stage, the hero encounters a divine being with godlike power. While the step is called "meeting with the goddess," the divine being can be a male god as well. Normally if it is a male hero, the divine is represented as a female and vice versa. This is because the purpose of the divine is for the hero to find balance in himself. In ancient myths, the combination of the masculine energy and the feminine energy represented completeness and godliness. If the divine is a goddess, they are usually depicted as a mother, sister, or lover figure. If the divine is a god, they are normally depicted as a father, brother, or lover figure. Occasionally the divine is represented by a creature from another race, such as an alien species. Even after the road of trials stage comes to an end, the hero and team still must face various trials, tests, and threshold guardians to reach the goddess. This divine character represents the power of femininity, which is the power of life and death, or good and evil. The divine character is extremely similar to the mentor, in the sense that they provide the hero with more information and tools that will help them with the latter half of the journey. However, the goddess figure normally is more powerful than the mentor and gives more effective tools to the hero. The goddess also generally shows up once the mentor has left or died. Moreover, the divine being normally gives the hero an impossible test that propels the hero into the crisis point of the story.

Lord of the Rings:

For the first story, Arwen serves as the lover goddess, while Elrond serves the fatherly god role. However in the overall trilogy (including *The Hobbit*), the character Galadriel acts as the motherly goddess. Each helps the hero in the absence of Gandalf, the main mentor figure in all of the stories. Additionally, they provide new information that propels them toward the crisis point. Throughout the various stories, Elrond has read secret maps, called together councils, healed various characters, and reassembled the Isildur's sword. Galadriel has provided shelter, information, visions of possible futures, advice, magic weapons, rope, and daggers. As ring bearers, they also possess immense power far greater than most beings in Middle Earth.

Star Wars:

In *A New Hope*, Leia serves in the sisterly goddess role. She helps the heroes escape the detention center once Obi Wan leaves, and we can assume she is the one that takes Luke to the secret rebel base on Yavin. It is also important to note that the character Mon Mothma represents the mother goddess in nearly all the Starwars films. She is the leader of the divine army (rebels), has great power as a senator, and provides the heroes tools for their mission (political support and various military space ships). However, if you look at the original trilogy as a whole, it is Yoda who acts as the goddess figure. He is far more powerful than Obi Wan and he completes Luke's training. He teaches Luke how to use the Force on a much grander scale, and he warns the hero about the lure of the dark side. Furthermore he tells Luke the history of his father, and that he has a sister.

Hunger Games:

In the first Hunger Games, Rue is the sisterly goddess. Once Katniss is in the arena, Rue helps the heroine defeat her attackers by pointing out the tracker jacker nest. Later Rue uses plants to heal Katniss' stings. She tells Katniss that Peeta is by the river, and she helps Katniss lay a trap at the cornucopia. In *Catching Fire*, Wiress acts in a similar fashion by informing the group that the arena is a giant clock. This is the critical information that allows them to survive the upcoming attacks and ultimately devise a plan of escape. To a lesser degree, Cinna can be seen as the brotherly divine figure, protecting Katniss through the Capitol's traditional presentations.

Harry Potter:

Throughout the multiple books, Harry encounters several goddesses--both good and evil. While Hermione acts as the first and primary goddess, Harry's mother, Professor McGonagall, and Ginny also serve in this role. Additionally, Bellatrix and Dolores Umbridge act as the evil manifestations of this divinity. The goddesses that help Harry, provide him wisdom, tools, magic totems, and enchantments to help him along his journeys. The fatherly god is Albus Dumbledore.

Stage 9: Woman as Temptress

In this stage, the hero faces a major temptation that threatens to lure him away from the journey. In old Arthurian myths, this was normally a woman that would tempt a knight from completing his quest. However, this stage can be any type of temptation from any type of character as long as it fits the theme of the story. Sexual temptation, greed, power, or breaking one's ethics are all examples of temptation motifs. While there may be several temptations throughout the story, this one normally happens near the midpoint and tries to take the hero away from the journey. This temptation usually happens as the hero and his team approach the innermost cave. Keep in mind, the hero's team mates can be affected by this temptation too.

Lord of the Rings:

Because the Lord of the Rings' theme revolves around power, there are multiple temptations throughout the trilogy. However, the one that fits the

Monomyth definition best is the scene where Frodo offers the Ring of Power to Galadriel. While the test seems to be for Galadriel, it affects the entire story. If she were to have accepted it, Frodo would have been free of his mission. But he would not have achieved hero status because the ring needed to be thrown into the fires of Mount Doom. Moreover, Galadriel would have most likely become consumed by the power of the ring, ultimately leading it back to Sauron. In the Two Towers, Gimli and Legolas try to persuade Aragorn not to fight at Helm's Deep. Faramir is tempted by the One Ring when he discovers Frodo has it. In *Return of the King*, Eowyn tries to talk Aragorn out of going to find the undead army.

Star Wars:

In Episode 4, once Han and Luke discover the Princess is in the detention center, Luke must tempt Han into saving her. While this doesn't distract the hero from his mission, it gives us insight into Han's motivations as a mercenary. This is critical to his character arc later in the story. In *Empire Strikes Back*, Yoda instructs Luke not to take his weapons in the cave, but he does anyway. He also warns Luke not to give into the Darkside. Lando charms Leia and Han into having dinner with Darth Vader. Another temptation comes from Vader when he urges Luke to join him so they can rule as father and son. In *Return of the Jedi*, Luke is tempted to leave the mission when he realizes Vader is on the ship they're passing. Later, Leia begs Luke not to turn himself in to Vader, by telling him to run far away from any place his father can sense him.

Hunger Games:

For Katniss, trust is a major theme throughout the books/films. Many of her temptations come when she has the upper hand on someone that could be an enemy, but she must learn to trust based on faith. For example, she could have killed Rue or Peeta multiple times in the first story. In the second, she has several chances to kill other victors, but decides to trust them, which turns out for the best in the long run.

Harry Potter:

In the *Philosopher's Stone*, Harry is tempted by the Mirror of Erised ("desire" spelled backward). According to Dumbledore, the mirror shows people what they want to see, and can drive men mad. Harry must force himself to stop believing the mirror's fantasy world where he sees his parents. If not, it will drive him insane. He must accept the real world and the fact that his parents are gone.

Stage 10: Atonement with the Father

This stage is very similar to the previous one. Again the hero comes in contact with a divine being. While the traditional title denotes a father figure, the character can be either male or female. If the hero is male, then normally he faces a god. If the heroine is female, then she will normally encounter a goddess. Unlike the previous stage where younger versions of the divine can represent the goddess/god, this stage requires a parental figure. Therefore the divine usually comes in the form of a father or a mother. Many times a duality may also be present. A positive animus and a negative animus depict the dichotomy of life. Often, the negative animus of this figure is represented as a monster, shadow, dragon, minotaur, or some other creature that evokes fear. The purpose of this stage is for the hero to understand the power of the gods. That is, that death, and pain, and all of the atrocities of life are natural, and normal. Despite the ugliness and unfairness of life, it is far beyond the judgement of mortals. The hero must realize this, and understand that they have no power over the horrific world they live in, and that they too are a monster in their own right. This generally marks the crisis, or midpoint of the story.

Lord of the Rings:

In *The Fellowship of the Ring*, Frodo and the fellowship must face a balrog, which is an ancient demon from past ages, a monster that represents the destructive power of the world. Even Gandalf, the mentor and father figure of the group, fears the creature. While he does everything he can to evade the creature, eventually he must face it head on. Despite its prodigious size and immense power, Gandalf holds it off (and, as we find out in later films, kills it). However, this momentary victory is bittersweet, because it comes with a great cost. Gandalf dies, sacrificing himself for the good of the group. Having just lost their father figure, the heroes try to make sense of his death.

In the second story, Aragorn convinces Theoden to ride out and face the horde of Uruk Hai face on. In the third installment, Ewen faces the

Witch-king of Angmar (negative animus--dragon battle) in order to save Theoden (positive animus--atonement), her father figure. For Aragorn, this is when he faces the cursed King of the Dead. Not only does this character represent a powerful parental figure, but also the negative animus (or shadow) of mankind. The Army of the Dead was cursed after breaking an oath, which is a foreshadowing of a later test Aragorn will have to face.

Star Wars:

In Episode 4, Obi Wan, Luke's father figure, faces Darth Vader. This is particularly interesting because Vader not only represents the shadow archetype, but he is also Luke's biological father. After Vader kills Obi Wan, Luke loses his father figure and must face the unfairness and reality of life. Later in Episode 5, Luke faces Vader himself. Once the Dark Lord defeats him by cutting off his hand, he informs Luke that he is his father. Not only is this a huge twist, but it gives Luke an entirely new perspective on the history of his father and the Skywalker mantle. In the third film Luke gives himself up to Vader. During their discussion, Luke senses the good in his father. At the end of the scene the Dark Lord of the Sith stares at his son's lightsaber, indicating his internal conflict. Since the original trilogy's overall story is about Anakin's redemption, this is atonement with the father is a reversal, where the father begins to atone with the son.

Hunger Games:

In order to get the medicine that can save Peeta, Katniss must sacrifice her own safety and go to an area swarming with Careers. During her attempt to get the medicine she is caught by Clove and nearly killed. However at the last minute Thresh kills Clove and spares Katniss for the kindness she showed Rue (the story's goddess figure). Not only is Thresh the mirror of Rue, but he represents great power as one of the strongest tributes in the game. Because of his mercy, Katniss is then able to retrieve the medicine and take it back to Peeta.

Harry Potter:

Harry goes into the dark forest and encounters a cloaked figure (Voldemort) drinking the blood of a unicorn. His scar begins to hurt and the creature looks as though it will attack Harry. Luckily a centaur saves him and the cowled figure runs off. The centaur tells him that the unicorn blood curses the drinker, but also allows a creature on the brink of death to live a little while longer. While Voldemort (the cloaked figure) may represent Harry's shadow, the unicorn represents the opposite, a powerful and magical creature with the ability to bring life. After hearing the news, Harry must contemplate the cruelty of life, in that such beauty can be destroyed by such evil.

Stage 11: Apotheosis

In this stage, the hero experiences momentary godhood, or apotheosis. In order to do that, most heroes must first go through an apostasis, that is, a dismemberment or removal of their old self. This can be a body part, weapon, tool, belief, a member of their team, or even someone from their past (or a variation). This removal serves as a sacrifice of the old self, making the hero vulnerable. This allows the hero to find balance within himself and start to heal. The hero realizes their own divinity for the first time. The hero is able to enter a state of godliness and wield a godlike power on a level only the divine can control. Whatever the hero loses should be symbolic of them releasing the psychological ties to their thematic flaw. Considering their character arc, this is serves as a major revelation to the hero. For the first time they can see past the lie that fuels their flaws, and tap into the truth. After this meaningful dismemberment, the hero will achieve apotheosis, or godhood, for a short period. This will be their first taste of the divine power that resides within them. From this point on, the hero will continually tap into the inner truth they've been missing, making them more and more powerful. By Final Battle Stage, the hero will have the power to completely tap into this divine power and defeat the antagonistic force.

Lord of the Rings:

For Frodo, the point of apotheosis is more subtle. Frodo's sacrifice is when he puts the ring on to evade the Uruk Hai. By making himself vulnerable to the All Seeing Eye of Sauron, he obtains the power of invisibility and escapes. Unfortunately this also allows the ring to start corrupting his soul. Shortly after this, Frodo leaves the fellowship and sets out on his own. In the Two Towers it is Aragorn who hits apotheosis. During the battle at Helm's Deep, the wall is breached, their army is cut in half and Haldir is killed by Uruk Hai. The Rohan soldiers retreat into the inner walls but it is only a matter of time before the enemy breaks in. Theoden loses faith and all hope seems lost until Aragorn convinces the King of Rohan to make a final charge against the forces of Saruman. This leads

Theoden into apotheosis, since he must sacrifice his life in a suicide run against Saruman's army, in order to give mankind hope. Since Aragorn's journey requires him to take up the mantle of the King, this is the first time he uses his Kingly power. This rally changes the course of battle, and the army of Rohan ends up winning. In the third installment, Aragon achieves momentary apotheosis when he challenges the King of the Dead and is able to hold his ground. He urges the oathbreakers to fulfill their vow, so that he can release them. Only the King of Gondor can make such demands. In order to do so, he had to leave Theoden and the Rohan army with Gimli and Legolas. Ewen also achieves apotheosis when she sacrifices herself to save Theoden and defeats the witch King of Angmar.

Star Wars:

In *A New Hope*, right after Vader kills Obi Wan, Luke achieves apotheosis. For most of his life he's been dependent on others, such as Uncle Owen and Aunt Beru. As his mentor, Luke relied on Obi Wan for guidance and protection. With the death of the Jedi master, the hero must learn to rely on himself and the Force (which represents intuition and the godlike power). Immediately he is one with the force. Not only does he shoot down several stormtroopers, but he destroys the blast door control panel on the other side of the hangar bay. This prevents Vader from chasing after them, and gives the hero and the team just enough time to escape the Death Star. Furthermore, from this point on, Luke is able to connect with Obi Wan through the force. In Episode five, Luke achieves apotheosis once he faces the Force shadow in the dark cave on Dagobah. After his failure in the cave, Luke begins to become stronger in the Force and receives visions of his friends in danger on Cloud City. In *Return of the Jedi*, Luke reaches apotheosis once he's given himself up to Darth Vader on Endor. The Dark Lord takes his lightsaber. After this sacrifice, Vader hints that Luke has become very powerful. For Luke, he finally realizes that there is still a part of Anakin Skywalker that is alive and that there may be a chance to redeem him.

Hunger Games:

For Katniss, this moment comes after she heals Peeta with the medicine. The two share a romantic moment in front of the Capitol cameras. This forces Katniss to be vulnerable and drop her defenses. It allows the whole world (of Panem) to see her personal life. For someone like Katniss, this is extremely difficult, but essential to get the citizens to empathize with her. With the viewers backing her, she holds power over the Gamemakers, forcing them to make decisions in her favor. While it's a momentary win, by the end of the story, she will wield this power to its greatest effect.

Harry Potter:

For this series, the hero achieves several moments of apotheosis, however for the sake of brevity, we will focus on the Philosopher's Stone. After speaking with Professor McGonagall, Harry and his friends find out that Dumbledore has been summoned away. Fearful that someone intends to steal the philosopher's stone, the trio takes things into their own hands and tries to catch the assumed thief. For Harry, this is important because he must learn that the adults won't always be there to take care of him. For the first time, he feels the power of responsibility. It's up to him and his friends to stop the philosipher's stone from being stolen.

Stage 12: The Ultimate Boon

The ultimate boon is an item of utmost importance to the story. Thematically, this represents a lesson or power that must be returned to the normal world in order to restore society. In primitive cultures the myth revolved around a hero who went into the wilderness to get food for the tribe. The animal represented life and death, both literally and figuratively. Without the food, the tribe would starve during the winter months. But also, on a deeper level, if the people in the society didn't work together, they would all perish. Sometimes the boon is a reward, or information. Other times it is an artifact of great power, or a weapon. And sometimes it can even be a healing elixir. Unlike other weapons, tools, and artifacts in the story, the boon symbolically represents a key aspect of the theme. In several stories, there is a physical boon, and a metaphysical boon. Other times, there are two opposing boons which represent the dichotomy of life. Many times the divine figure from Stage 8 is the person who sends the hero on a quest to retrieve this boon. The hero and their team believe the mission to be an impossible task because it requires them to approach the innermost cave and face the parental figure from Stage 10. A perfect example is the Wizard of Oz sending Dorothy and her friends to get the Wicked Witch's broomstick. This requires the motley crew to infiltrate the dark dungeon and defeat the Wicked Witch.

In many stories, the hero already possesses the boon in physical form, but is tasked to guard it. Later, in the climax battle, the hero must unlock the boon's metaphysical power to bring balance back to society. A good example of this is the Matrix of Power from the 1984 Transformers the Movie. After Optimus Prime dies, the Autobots must prevent the Decepticons from taking the Matrix. Ultimately Hot Rod uses the boon to defeat Galvatron and destroy Unicron. No matter what kind of boon it is, the primary goal of the hero is to return the boon to the normal world in order to restore society. In modern stories the boon is normally achieved/retrieved after the dragon battle and apotheosis. Occasionally it may precede these events or happen concurrently.

Lord of the Rings:

The Ring of Power is the ultimate boon in Lord of the Rings. Frodo's goal is to prevent the evil forces of Mordor from taking the ring, and ultimately destroying it in Mount Doom. This mission is given to Frodo and his companions multiple times. First by Elrond at the Council of Elrond, then again by Galadriel in Lothlorien. Several other characters and scenes repeat the importance of this item. Since the theme itself deals with power and its ultimate corruptibility, it only makes sense that the ring is a symbol of power and corruption.

Aragorn is a secondary hero and has his own quest with his own boon, the Shards of Narsil. They are the broken pieces of Isildur's sword, which thematically represents the broken lines of kingship and authority. Aragorn must earn the right of kingship through a series of tests. This mission is given to him by Elrond and reemphasized by Galadriel. Ultimately Elrond is convinced to use the magic of the elves to fix the sword. Renamed to Andruil (Flame of the West), Aragorn uses the sword to earn the allegiance of the undead army, and ultimately reclaim his birthright, for only the true King of Gondor can wield the sword, and redeem the oath breakers from their eternal hell. Metaphorically, both boons represent lessons for mankind.

Star Wars:

In Star Wars, there is a physical boon and a metaphysical boon. The physical boon is the plans of the Death Star. Because of Luke and his friends, the Rebellion is able to find a weakness in the planet killing machine. The metaphysical boon is the force, which represents intuition. Both boons are complementary to each other when considering the theme. The story's theme is to trust in one's intuition rather than relying on, or succumbing to, a machine-like system. The vulnerability of machines is that they lack human intuition. Thus, Luke uses the Force to capitalize on the Death Star's vulnerability. In the later films, Vader is redeemed by finding his humanity once again.

Hunger Games:

In Hunger Games, there are two contrasting boons which depict the dichotomy of the theme. First is the medicine Katniss must retrieve to save Peeta. This is the elixir of life, both literally and figuratively. Not only does it save Peeta in the real world, but metaphorically, Katniss must sacrifice her safety to save another tribute. This is in blatant disregard to the underlying idea of the Games, which is that everyone is out for themselves. The second boon is Nightlock, a poisonous berry that is fatal when eaten. This is the elixir of death, both literally and figuratively. When the Gamemasters attempt to make Peeta and Katniss turn on each other, the two must decide who will die a physical death. Peeta urges Katniss to kill him, so she can go back to her family. However Katniss realizes that if she allows Peeta to die, she wouldn't be able to live with herself. Instead the two decide to sacrifice themselves, knowing it's far better to die on their own terms, than to allow the Capitol to take their integrity. This gives them power over death, for they know that real death does not take place in the body, but rather in the heart and mind of the individual.

Harry Potter:

The philosopher's stone is the first boon in the series and it serves as a false boon. Its power allures because it allows the user to prolong their life. However, only those who don't wish to use it can obtain it. That is why Harry is given the philosopher's stone. Even though he was looking for it, he had no intention of using it. Voldemort, on the other hand, wishes to use the stone's power to restore himself. This speaks to the theme of the first book and the series in general. Just as the unicorn blood and the stone's power are temporary, so too is life. Physical immortality is a myth. Yet Voldemort wishes to live forever, and therefore he will stop at nothing to achieve immortality. He has no qualms about using dark magic and killing others to get what he wants. Love on the other hand is the true boon, and is a power that lasts forever. That is why we see Harry sacrifice himself time and time again to help those he cares about.

Recap

As mentioned earlier, the Initiation Act serves as a testing ground for the hero and his allies. The purpose of the Initiation Act is to test the hero and the team with multiple obstacles that gradually build in difficulty over time. It introduces key characters such as the shapeshifter, trickster, and the shadow. The hero will get their first glimpse of the special world, and its difficulties. The hero experiences death and sacrifice on a much deeper level than he did in the Separation Act. The Initiation Act is split into two sections: trials and transformation. During the trials the hero will face a series of tests that teach him valuable lessons. After these trials, the hero will go through the transformative stages in order to find balance in his life and reach his full potential. At the end of this act, either the hero or the shadow will have taken possession of the boon.

Action Items

Take a moment to write down the answers to these questions:

- TRIALS: What obstacles can you put in your hero's way to help him learn lessons about the special world, but more importantly, things that will teach him how to overcome his flaw? (While on the exterior these can be man vs man or man vs nature conflicts, they must metaphorically represent inner changes happening in the character arc.)
    - ☐ Meteors
    - ☐ Trolls
    - ☐ Goblins
    - ☐ Dark knights
    - ☐ Mountains
    - ☐ Woods
    - ☐ Tunnels
- GODDESS: Who will best represent the divine? The divine usually is the opposite sex of the hero (or an asexual alien creature such as Yoda). Sometimes the divine can be malevolent, like the three Stygian Witches in

Clash of the Titans. Like the mentor they will provide more tools or information to the hero.

- ☐ Old man/woman
- ☐ Witch/warlock/wizard
- ☐ Alien creature/species
- ☐ Young child/spritely creature
- ☐ Crazy person

- IMPOSSIBLE TASK: What impossible task will force the hero to obtain the boon? The more your boon is related to the hero's flaw, the clearer your theme will be.
  - ☐ Steal elixir/tool
  - ☐ Save someone
  - ☐ Pull sword from stone
  - ☐ Retrieve item of great power
  - ☐ Kill monster to obtain special power

- TEMPTATION: What temptations will the hero and their team face while on the impossible task? The more these temptations are related to the hero's flaw, the clearer your theme will be. Usually the hero temptation makes them consider quitting their mission.
  - ☐ Promotion

- [ ] Money
- [ ] Lust
- [ ] Love
- [ ] Power
- [ ] Cowardice
- [ ] Responsibility/Duty

- FATHER FIGURE: What monstrous power must the hero confront in order to obtain the boon? Normally this is a parental figure, or a creature of great power like a god.
  - [ ] Dragon
  - [ ] Monster
  - [ ] Minotaur
  - [ ] God
  - [ ] Demon
  - [ ] Angel
  - [ ] Demigod
  - [ ] Parent/Grandparent

- TASTE OF DIVINITY: How can your hero show a display of their newfound power? This usually happens when they decide to deny their flaw/crutch and accept an inner/sacred truth.

The closer this power is tied to their flaw, the clearer your theme will become.

- ☐ Able to see things clearly
- ☐ See the future/past
- ☐ Use magic
- ☐ Transform
- ☐ Call upon an inner strength
- ☐ Give love
- ☐ Resist old habits
- ☐ Teleport
- ☐ Fight

Return: The Third and Final Act of the Hero's Journey

As you know, the Hero's Journey is broken up into three main acts: Separation, Initiation, and Return. In this chapter, we're discussing the third and final act of the Monomyth, the "Return" act. During this act the hero will have to face the antagonistic force for the last time in a climactic battle. He will be tested once again, but the stakes will be much higher. He must use all of the lessons learned in the Initiation Act in order to achieve victory. Normally this requires a major sacrifice on the hero's part. In most cases the hero must overcome their major flaw, and in some cases this requires them to actually become a martyr for the cause. Only through death of the old self can the hero be reborn anew. Once the sacrifice is made, the hero reaches a divine state and has the power to revitalize the society. From that point, they have mastered both the ordinary world and the special world, bringing balance to both. Ultimately this frees the hero from fear of his past, and allows him to move on toward the future with boldness.

Purpose of the Return Act

In many ways, the Return Act is the most meaningful. Not only is this where the climax happens, but it provides the hero meaning to the journey and should deliver a lesson to the audience. The purpose of the Return Act is for the hero to bring the boon back to the normal world. It provides the hero's final test, normally in the form of a climactic battle, to prove he has retained all of the lessons in the narrative. The hero experiences death on the deepest level possible, which is martyrdom. Finally this act ties up loose ends and returns the hero back to the ordinary world, but with a renewed sense of purpose.

Return Stages

In order to achieve the above narrative goals, the storyteller must make use of the six stages in the Return Act. Below is a list for easy reference (continuing from the Initiation Act):

13. Refusal of the Return

14. The Magic Flight

15. Rescue from Without

16. The Crossing of the Return Threshold

17. Master of Two Worlds

18. Freedom to Live

In the following chapters we'll analyze these stages in more detail.

Stage 13: Refusal of the Return

This stage is similar to the Refusal of the Call, in that it shows an unwillingness on the hero's part to accept the change happening in his life. Having been in the special world for so long, the hero becomes accustomed to the new rules and does not desire to leave. Perhaps they have become addicted to their newfound powers, or lustful of new relationships, or fearful of what might happen if they go back. Or perhaps they find the normal world too boring compared to the adventure they have experienced. In any event, once again the refusal proves to the audience that your hero is still human and has the same psychological issues as we all do. In mythology, the refusal was a return to the normal world. Even now, this is the purest and most potent use of this metaphysical stage. However, in contemporary stories, the refusal is sometimes represented with the hero or his team avoiding a dangerous place, such as the villain's lair.

Lord of the Rings:

At the end of *Fellowship of the Ring*, Frodo attempts to give Aragorn the ring. Not only is this a temptation test for Aragorn, but Frodo is refusing his mission to take the ring back to Mordor alone. In the Two Towers, the Ents don't want to go to battle with Isengard. Only after Merry and Pippin coax Treebeard into going south do the ancient beings change their minds. Theoden refuses to "risk open war" and decides to fortify at Helm's Deep. In the final story, both Sam and Frodo worry about how they will get through Mordor and to Mount Doom. The King of the Dead does not initially accept Aragorn's proposal to release them from their eternal damnation.

Star Wars:

In Star Wars this happens after Leia gives the Death Star plans to the rebels. Luke approaches Han to see if he's going on the trench run. Han tells Luke he's not going because he doesn't want to get killed and would rather be alive to use his reward. Han then suggests that Luke should come with him and Chewbacca. Disappointed, Luke scolds him and heads off to battle. In the next episode, Yoda tries to convince Luke to stay on Dagobah to complete his Jedi training, rather than rescuing his friends on Cloud City. In *Return of the Jedi*, Leia tells Luke to run away from Vader rather than confront him. If we consider Darth Vader (Anakin Skywalker) as the overall protagonist of the original trilogy, then this stage happens when Luke insists that there is still good in his father and urges him to return to the light side. Vader denies it, but deep down he knows it to be true.

Hunger Games:

Katniss and Peeta must go back to the cornucopia to beat the rest of the victors. Katniss in particular isn't sure how she'll handle a confrontation with Thresh, since he saved her life. The same holds true with Foxface, as she doesn't really mean her harm either. Katniss also frets about how to defeat Cato, who is perhaps the strongest Career in the game. Most importantly, Katniss' main goal is to keep Peeta alive. For all of these reasons, she does not want to return to the cornucopia.

Harry Potter:

When Harry, Hermione, and Ron set out to stop Professor Quirrell from stealing the philosopher's stone, Neville, a friend and fellow Gryffindor student, attempts to stop the trio from breaking the rules. While Neville's intentions are based in loyalty, and his argument is logical, it provides the psychological refusal to Harry and his friends as to why they should abandon their mission. Even at the end of the story, Professor Dumbledore commends Neville for his actions, thus placing Gryffindor House as the winner of the Hogwarts trophy.

Stage 14: The Magic Flight

Although sometimes depicted as actual flying, this stage actually refers to a pursuit or evasion. Many times the hero and villain are racing against each other in order to return the power of the boon to the normal world. The "magic" can be special technology, or an ethereal transcendence, or sometimes a method that the hero cannot do himself (piloting a ship), while the purest form is when the hero is pursued by attackers. In contemporary fiction, this stage can also be the antagonist being chased by the hero. Sometimes, instead of a chase, this stage depicts heroes or antagonists evading obstacles while in pursuit of the boon. Either the hero is trying to stop the antagonistic force from releasing the negative power of the boon on society, or the antagonistic force is attempting to prevent the hero from releasing the positive power of the boon to society.

Lord of the Rings:

In the *Fellowship of the Ring*, the fellowship is pursued by Uruk Hai. Frodo uses the one ring to evade them, while the others fight. In the second story, Aragorn and the army of Rohan must evade the Warg riders while the townspeople get to the safety of Helm's Deep. Frodo and Sam must hide from the Nazgul. In *Return of the King*, Frodo and Sam are chased by orcs, Gollum, and the Ever Seeing Eye in their attempt to get to Mount Doom. After urging the Army of the Dead to fight with them, Aragorn, Legolas, and Gimli must escape the cave before it collapses on them.

Star Wars:

Luke and the rebels race to destroy the Death Star, as Vader and Tarkin attempt to blow up the rebel base. Each team of X-wings are chased by TIE fighters while having to evade turbo cannons during the trench run. The rebel pilots evade several of the attackers, but Darth Vader leads the trench defense team, killing many of Luke's allies. In Episode 5, Han is frozen in carbonite. Boba Fett takes Han before the others can free him. Leia, Lando, Chewbacca and the droids must evade stormtroopers to get to the Millennium Falcon, while at the same time Luke chases after them, trying to save his friends. In the third movie, Wicket the Ewok distracts the scout troopers by stealing a speeder bike. Meanwhile Lando and Admiral Ackbar are evading Star Destroyers and Death Star blasts in the space battle above.

Hunger Games:

Katniss and Peeta are chased by mutant dogs while they attempt to get back to the cornucopia. In the book these creatures are made from the DNA of the dead victors, so they are haunting on many levels. They eventually evade the monsters by climbing to the top of the structure. At the same time, Cato, the only remaining tribute, is waiting for them at the top in order to kill them and win the Hunger Games.

Harry Potter:

When they find out Hagrid has told others how to get past Fluffy, Harry and his friends race to find out who killed the unicorn and is trying to steal the philosopher's stone. Unbeknownst to them, Professor Quirrell, under the command of Voldemort, is racing to find the philosopher's stone by using the magic mirror. Voldemort wants the power of the stone, so he may return to his full power and live forever.

Stage 15: Rescue from Without

Many times the hero needs assistance crossing the return threshold, usually because the hero is weak, injured, or otherwise incapable. This help normally comes from an unlikely character - usually someone the hero has taken for granted, underestimated, or considered beneath him. Oftentimes this can be a sidekick or ally who left during the refusal of the return, or perhaps someone the hero had an argument with. After receiving help, the hero learns humility, which is necessary to temper his newfound powers.

Lord of the Rings:

In the first story, Boromir helps Merry and Pippin by fighting off several of the Uruk Hai. All three of these characters also act as a distraction for Frodo while he escapes. In the second story, Aragorn is saved by Brego, the wild stallion of Rohan, who takes him back to Helm's Deep. In the third movie, the Army of the Dead save Aragorn and his friends from the Corsair ships, and later help defeat the

Easterlings and remaining Mordor armies at Gondor. This is an unexpected move by the undead army because they were oathbreakers in their last lives.

Samwise Gamgee is the epitome of the metaphysical exchange that should happen during this stage. In the second story, Sam pushes Frodo out of the way, just before a Nazgul snatches the ring bearer. He also achieves a moment of apotheosis in the third story when he faces and defeats Shelob, the giant spider. Thematically, Sam's mission is one of support. In order for the gardener from Hobbiton to achieve his fullest potential, he must learn to fight for the hero when the hero cannot fight for himself. These scenes serve two purposes. First, Sam achieves momentary godlike status. Second, he saves Frodo from the jaws of death. In the third movie, Sam rescues Frodo from the orcs and Uruk Hai that were planning on taking him to the All Seeing Eye. As a simple minded gardener from Hobbiton, Sam is continually taken for granted, and Frodo is continually humbled by his friend's loyalty and bravery.

In some ways, the Eagles also represent this stage in Tolkien's writing. They consistently appear around this point in the story to assist the hero (this happens in *The Hobbit* as well). According to lore, these majestic birds normally didn't interfere with the wars of orcs and men, so in that regard, every time they appear, it is an unlikely occurrence.

Star Wars:

In *A New Hope,* this moment happens when Han Solo returns and saves Luke from Vader. Both Luke and Princess Leia have a newfound respect for their smuggler friend, whom they considered a mercenary up until this point. For Han, who is a hero in his own right, this is his moment of martyrdom and marks a full character arc on his behalf. In *The Empire Strikes Back*, Lando Calrissian fulfills this role, by saving Leia, Chewbacca, the droids, and eventually Luke. In the *Return of the Jedi*, Wicket and the Ewoks assist the rebels in fighting the Imperial forces on Endor.

Hunger Games:

At this point in the story Katniss is worried about how to return with Peeta. While she knows Cato is a formidable enemy, she frets over having to face Thresh and Foxface. Throughout the games, she's run into both of these tributes and does not wish to do either of them harm. Yet when her and Peeta go hunting they split up. When she hears the cannons go off, Katniss assumes he's been killed. Only after searching for him, does she discover that Foxface died from nightlock (the negative boon).This is a rescue from without on several levels. First, with Foxface dead, there's one less tribute to deal with. Second, Katniss no longer has to deal with the moral dilemma of killing another tribute in cold blood. Third, Foxface's death acts similar to a sacrifice, giving Katniss an idea on how to defeat Cato. So while Foxface may have technically been a rival, in the end, her existence leads them closer to a way to actually win the games. Thresh's death is very similar to Foxface's in the first two regards. Additionally, it gives Katniss and Peeta just a momentary heads-up that something bad is coming. Anything that could kill Thresh must be extremely formidable. This tiny warning is just enough for them to ready their defenses and face the mutant dogs.

Harry Potter:

While investigating Professor Snape, the trio discovers that he was actually trying to save Harry during the quidditch tournament. They discover that he was using a spell to keep Harry from getting hurt. This is unexpected, as all three of the young wizards assumed that Professor Snape is evil and secretly working for Voldemort. While we won't analyze the entire series, it is of note that Professor Snape fulfills this role multiple times throughout the Harry Potter series.

Stage 16: The Crossing of the Return Threshold

Once the hero has returned, they must learn how to integrate their new knowledge into the normal world. This normally means fighting through more obstacles, which build and build until they culminate in the final climax. Everything leads the hero toward facing their ultimate enemy one last time in an epic battle/fight/argument at the climax of the narrative. Many times, crossing the return threshold causes heavy casualties for the hero and his team. Friends may be lost or killed in battle. Sometimes the antagonist suffers heavy losses as well. By the end of this stage, the hero will come face to face with the main lieutenant of the antagonistic force (usually the shadow archetype or contagonist).

Lord of the Rings:

This is where Frodo and Sam get in the boat and set out toward Mordor in the first book. Aragorn and the rest of the fellowship must fight their way through hordes of Uruk Hai. Boromir is shot with several arrows by the enemy commander. However, just before the creature kills him, Aragorn comes to his aid. In the second book, Aragorn convinces Theoden to ride out to face the enemy army in what seems to be a suicide rally. A small band of men on horses take on several hundred Uruk Hai. The Ents take on Isengard, knowing that they may face their ultimate doom. In the third story, Aragorn and the armies of men approach Mordor in order to distract Sauron and to buy Frodo and Sam time to destroy the One Ring. After many losses in the Battle for Gondor, it is difficult for Aragorn and the other heroes to confront the enemy's gates. Aragorn gives a speech to the Army of Men, encouraging them to hold strong.

Star Wars:

After Han knocks Vader off course, Luke is free to fire his shot at the Death Star. This is an extremely difficult feat and other more experienced pilots have already missed. Luke activates his targeting system and prepares to fire. In the meantime the Death Star targeter informs Governor Tarkin that they are within range of the rebel base. He instructs the Imperials to fire when ready. In Episode 5, this is where Luke chases after his friends, evades stormtroopers, and escapes the carbonite chamber. The stage ends with Luke facing Vader mano a mano. In the third movie, Han and the rest of the rebels must blow up the shield generator. Meanwhile in space, Lando is facing Star Destroyers at point blank range, while Luke confronts the Emperor face to face.

Hunger Games:

Katniss and Peeta must climb the cornucopia in order to evade the mutant mutts. This proves more difficult than it seems when they find Cato is also on top of the structure. Katniss and Peeta struggle against Cato, however in the end, the Career locks Peeta into a chokehold atop the cornucopia. Katniss shoots an arrow through Cato's hand, which allows Peeta to push him over the edge. The mutant dogs finish off Cato. The two believe they have won, but the Gamemakers, who are the real antagonistic force, inform them that they must kill each other.

Harry Potter:

After discovering Professor Snape was trying to protect them, not hurt them, they rush to confront Professor Quirrell. While in pursuit of Professor Quirrell, Harry and his friends evade Fluffy, the three-headed dog. Then they are ensnared by a large plant and must use fire magic to escape. Lastly they face a life-sized magical chess set. Each serves as a threshold guardian. Ron sacrifices himself to defeat the chess pieces and allow Harry to pass through to the final chamber. Hermione stays behind to look after Ron and the hero faces Quirrell, who he soon discovers is acting as a vessel for Voldemort.

Stage 17: Master of Both Worlds

This is the climax of the narrative. Everything has built up to this point of the story, the final confrontation. Normally, the hero must confront the major antagonist and overcome their major flaw. Most often, this requires the hero to become a martyr for the cause. Having given the ultimate sacrifice, the hero is resurrected. Normally, the hero enters a god-like state. Powers become fully realized, and having incorporated the lessons from the journey into the normal world, the hero can now use their powers without hindrance. The hero uses power to bring balance to both worlds.

Lord of the Rings:

In the first book, Frodo and Sam set out on their own, knowing that they will probably die along the journey. Aragorn faces the Uruk Hai commander one on one. He nearly dies multiple times, but ends up decapitating the monster. In the second story, Frodo and Sam face a Nazgul in Los Giliath. Frodo nearly gives the ring to the wraith, but Sam pushes his friend out of the way. Later he reminds Frodo why their mission is important. The Ents release the river and defeat Isengard and the Evil wizard Saruman. In the third book, Frodo struggles with Gollum, Sam, and himself while approaching the fires of Mount Doom. Eventually Frodo chooses to live a simple life rather than feel the power of the ring one last time. This heroic act allows Aragorn and his friends to defeat the armies of Mordor.

Star Wars:

In *A New Hope*, this is the moment Luke turns off his targeting system and uses the Force to shoot the crippling blow to the Death Star. In Episode 5, Luke meets Darth Vader face to face. After an epic duel and the loss of his hand, Luke learns Vader is his father. Rather than join the Dark Side, the hero stoically sacrifices himself by letting go and falling into the abyss below. In the third installment, Luke resists the Emperor and the allure of the Dark Side. He sacrifices himself rather than kill his father or give up his sister. Vader also has a redemptive moment where he destroys the Emperor and sacrifices himself so his son can live.

Hunger Games:

After defeating Cato and the mutant dogs, the Gamemakers recant on their deal to allow two victors from the same district to win. Katniss and Peeta are told they must fight to the death in order to leave the arena alive. Rather than "lose" themselves or each other to the games, the star-crossed lovers resolve to sacrifice themselves and eat the deadly Nightlock plant. This undermines the entire purpose of the Hunger Games, and ultimately gives Katniss and Peeta an existential victory.

Harry Potter:

Voldemort confronts Harry and tells him to look into the magic mirror so he can find the philosopher's stone. Little does the antagonist know, the stone is actually in Harry's pocket. While the stone does give long life to its master, only those who do not wish to use it can possess it. Harry tricks Voldemort initially, but eventually Voldemort attempts to use his dark magic against the boy wizard. In a sudden turn of events, Voldemort is vanquished by some mysterious power. Later, Dumbledore explains that it was his mother's love that defeated Voldemort. Her sacrifice covered him in the most powerful magic in the world, love. Not even black magic could penetrate the power of his mother's love for him.

Stage 18: Freedom to Live

In this stage, the hero is free to return to the normal world. However, something is different about them on the inside. The hero has taken on a new form. They are no longer the old person that clings to their flaw/crutch, but rather reborn. Sometimes this means the hero takes on a new title, position, or station in life. Other times, this means the hero is looked at with respect from those who shunned him before the journey. This is because the hero is the embodiment of the lessons they have learned. They can now go about life free of fear or pain from the old antagonistic force.

Lord of the Rings:

In the first book, Frodo and Sam trek toward Mordor with a new sense of purpose. They are free of the burden of other members who may be tempted to take the One Ring (as Boromir attempted to do). Before Boromir dies, he is redeemed through his actions and words, thus allowing him to enter the afterlife "free of sin," and a hero. With Frodo and Sam on their own, Aragorn, Legolas, and Gimli are free to track down the Uruk Hai and save Merry and Pippin. In the second story, Rohan is free to return to Edoras and live in peace, without fear of Isengard attacking. Theoden has proven himself as king, and the others have proven themselves as battleworn heroes. The Ents have saved the remainder of the forest from the evil wizard, Saruman. Since Merry and Pippin were critical to the success of this battle, they are now heroes in their own rights. When Faramir releases Frodo and Sam, they are free to continue on their mission to Mordor. In the third book, the world of man is free from Sauron's evil machinations. Frodo and Sam are rescued by the eagles. Aragorn is crowned king. He is also free to explore his relationship with Arwen, the elven princess. Middle Earth is safe. Each of the Hobbits return to Hobbiton as heroes of middle earth.

Star Wars:

In Episode 4, the rebels are safe from the destructive power of the Death Star. Han and Luke are rewarded for their bravery and become heroes of the

New Republic. In the end of the second movie, Luke is free of self doubt. Since he's confronted the Dark Lord, he no longer fears Vader. The truth is also freeing, in that Luke now knows the real story of his father. In the third movie, Vader defeats the Emperor, thus redeeming himself to his son and his old self. The galaxy is free from the Empire, and the heroes are free to help rebuild the republic. Luke, Han, Leia, Lando, Chewbacca and the droids are saviors of the galaxy.

Hunger Games:

Just before the star-crossed lovers eat the Nightlock, the Gamemakers change the rules again, and declare both Katniss and Peeta victors. Because they survived, the two go back to the Capitol as victors of the Hunger Games. Eventually they return to District 12, where they can see their families and return to life the way it was. Only now, they have unlimited rations and large houses to live in.

Harry Potter

Voldemort is defeated because Harry is protected by the most powerful magic in the world, a force that the villain could never comprehend: unconditional love. Later Dumbledore explains to Harry that because of his mother's love and sacrifice, Voldemort was unable to hurt the young wizard. Harry returns home knowing he is a wizard and that he has friends. Best of all, he knows his parents loved him very much.

Recap

As mentioned earlier, the Return Act is the final act of the Hero's Journey and is comprised of six distinct stages. During these stages the hero must return the boon back to the normal world in order to revitalize society. Not all heroes will wish to return to the normal world, and sometimes they may need help getting back. Along their way, they may be chased and they will face many challenges which will culminate in a final climactic confrontation with the major antagonistic force. In order to succeed, the hero will have to make a sacrifice which normally requires them to overcome a major flaw. After defeating the major antagonist, the hero will be free to live in both worlds without fear, as a key member of society.

Action Items

Take a moment to write down the answers to these questions:

- REFUSAL: Your hero or someone on his team should not want to return to the normal world.

Who is best suited to serve this role? Why don't they wish to return?

- [ ] Temptation
- [ ] Other obligations
- [ ] Addicted to the special world
- [ ] Duty

- PURSUIT: What will the hero and antagonist race against each other for?
  - [ ] Obtain hand of the same woman in marriage
  - [ ] Save the world
  - [ ] Destroy a weapon
  - [ ] Power over a person
  - [ ] Money

- RESCUE: Who will save your character in a moment of vulnerability?
  - [ ] Old friend
  - [ ] Someone the hero got into an argument with
  - [ ] Someone the hero takes for granted
  - [ ] Someone the hero thought was an enemy (fake opponent)
  - [ ] Someone the hero thought littl

- [ ] Someone the hero thought was dead
- [ ] Someone who left during the refusal
- [ ] Handicapped character
- [ ] Pet or sidekick
- [ ] Rival
- [ ] Fool
- [ ] Klutz
- [ ] Cutthroat/mercenary

- **CASUALTIES:** What casualties will the hero and team encounter in order to face the antagonist head on?
  - [ ] Death of teammates
  - [ ] Pain and suffering of loved ones
  - [ ] Loss of friends or meaningful objects
  - [ ] The love of a friend, child, or spouse
  - [ ] Their reputation is tarnished
  - [ ] Money is lost
  - [ ] Possessions taken away

- **MASTERY:** How will your hero overcome their flaw in order to defeat the antagonistic force?
  - [ ] Sacrifice
  - [ ] Forgiveness
  - [ ] Change of mind

- ☐ Acceptance
- ☐ Love
- FREEDOM: How can you show your hero back in his normal world, but changed? His flaw/crutch no longer has the same power it once did.
    - ☐ He finally musters the courage to talk to his crush
    - ☐ When she gets stressed, she doesn't reach for alcohol
    - ☐ She chooses her daughter's play over a meeting at work
    - ☐ Doesn't let the bully take his lunch money
    - ☐ Answers the phone this time

Closing Remarks

If you're still with me, congratulations! You've reached the end of this journey.

As I mentioned before, the Monomyth is the historical storytelling tool that mankind has used for centuries. It acts as a guide, helping us write our story along the way. The structure is split up into three main acts, Separation, Initiation, and Return. Each act is comprised of six distinct stages. Through the journey, the hero is thrust from the ordinary world into the special world. After a series of trials and external conflicts he learns internal lessons that change him on a psychological level. He learns how to overcome his flaws and returns to the ordinary world in order to revitalize society. By the end of the story, the journey has changed the hero. They no longer cling to their flaws, but rather work through problems using a new way of thought.

I hope this book helped you gain a greater understanding of the Monomyth. The examples provided demonstrate fundamental aspects of the

Hero's Journey. While there are many more advanced steps and features to learn, you should now have a basic understanding of how the Monomyth fits in modern storytelling.

Now that you're familiar with the stages of the Monomyth, imagine how you can apply it to your own stories. How can you add deeper meaning that will resonate with your readers? Perhaps there are areas of your narrative that could be bolstered with this new knowledge? Consider the sections of your story that you've been stuck on. Can any of the stages, examples, or action items help you get past that writer's block which hindered you in the past? My hope is that you use this book as a roadmap, referencing it if you get lost or stuck in your story, and that ultimately you can share your gift with the world.

If you found this information helpful and informative, please share a review so that other storytellers can benefit from the information. If you wish to find out more about the Monomyth, look me up on all of the social media platforms where I share videos, blogs, and courses on the topic.

Thank You From Story Ninjas

Story Ninjas Publishing would like to thank you for reading our book. We hope you found value in this product and would love to hear your feedback. Please provide your constructive criticism in a review on Amazon. Also feel free to share this book through the various social media platforms.

Other Books by Story Ninjas

Story Ninjas Publishing hopes you enjoyed this book. Below are some other products you may be interested in.

Dark Tales

By S. Cary

Summary: Three spooky, spine-tingling, creepy short stories. This collection contains 'Hunting With Grandpa', 'Hide', and 'The Return'.

Dark Tales 2

By S. Cary

Summary: Planning a cabin trip? Going hunting? Looking for stories to tell around the campfire? Or maybe you want to spook your friends this weekend? This is the book for you. Dark Tales is the second installment of tantalizing tales from Story Ninjas. In this collection you'll find SEVEN scary stories to tell around the campfire. From killer clowns to viral parasites, this anthology has all kinds of haunting stories to make your spine tingle. What happens when a group of college students come back from a cabin trip only to find mysterious photos on their phones? Or what about an author that must make her story go viral in order to avoid a gruesome death? Maybe you would prefer to read about a boyfriend who takes his ex girlfriend to the same bridge his best friend died just a year ago? All of these stories and more await you in Dark Tales Volume 2.

Shadow Magic

By S. Cary

Summary: Ali is an adventurous girl that lives with her annoying little sister, Gabby. They are two typical sisters with a typical sibling rivalry. They live in a typical house in a typical neighborhood.

Or so she thinks…

Little does Ali know, magical forces beyond her wildest dreams live in the woods near their backyard. One day while playing out back, the girls get into a fight and Ali storms off. She's fed up with Gabby. The little runt is always messing with her stuff. But, when

Gabby goes missing the next morning, Ali sets out on an adventure that will not only change the course of her life, but save the world from utter destruction.

Angelion: Descent

By Brennien Coker

Summary: Angels are real. Given the task of saving a human life, a band of angels traverse the spiritual plans. Leaving the comfort of Angelion, the angel city, they are thrust into a spiritual war. Based on the angels of the Bible, Angelion tells the story of everyday life of angels.

The Fuzz

By Brennien Coker

Summary: This is a lighthearted series of a man named Sam Duffy, who just so happens to be a fan of crime fighting TV shows. He has watched every episode of his favorite TV show "The Fuzz" three times. There is nothing noteworthy or special about Sam. That is of course except for the fact that one day Sam awoke to find himself in "The Fuzz", in the role of the lead Detective Samuel Barnes. Unable to return to his old life Sam decides to solve the case under the guise of a real detective. He soon finds out that watching a detective solve a case and actually solving the case are totally different. However, Sam has one major advantage. He is inside a rerun episode, and he knows exactly who the dog bomber is.

Blind: A Short Story Anthology

By Suzanne Sherwood and Josh Coker

Summary: Blind is a collection of four short stories. Each narrative focuses on characters that come across new insights in their personal lives. The main story revolves around a blind man named Zane, who is given the opportunity to see for the first time in his life. The question is, does he really want to open his eyes to see the new world that awaits him. The second story, When Worlds Collide, is about a boy named Akbar. He is trying to return the magic rock to his people while also evading the monsters nearby. The third story, The Great Smoky Mountains, is about an older couple that come to an important realization late in life. The fourth story, Monster Madness, is about a character who has decided to clean out their closet. Little does he know, the process is much harder than anticipated.

About Face

By Josh Coker

Summary: When it comes to military transitions books, veterans are given a firehose of instructions. How to dress, how to write a resume, how to give an interview, blah, blah,blah... This information overload, can overwhelm military members to the point of inaction. About Face provides quick tips that cut through the BS, so veterans can take action immediately. Once you've finished reading these badass tips, you'll be able to identify common pitfalls that most military members make, and change course before it's too late. Not only that, but veterans will be able to navigate the unknown jungles of the corporate sector with confidence and ease. Whether you're active duty planning to get out, a veteran who's already transitioned, a family member, or a supervisor who wishes to assist your troops, *About Face* will give you the tools you need to make decisions going forward.

Ollie's Scary Space Adventure

By Josh Coker

Illustrations by Selene Cook

Summary: Ollie is an adventurous boy that just moved from a big city to a small town. It's the day before Halloween and he misses his old friends, so he takes his dog for a walk. Along the way he meets Jesse, the next door neighbor. She shows Ollie all of the best spots to get candy, but warns him to stay away from the house on top of the hill because it's haunted. Apparently it belonged to a mad scientist. Ollie thanks Jessie for the information, and returns to his house, excited to have met someone new.

The next day, Ollie takes his sister trick-or-treating in the hopes he'll get to see Jesse again. Little does he know, he's about to embark on the wildest adventure of his life! Follow Ollie and his friends as they go where no trick-or-treater has ever gone before... SPACE!

Flight of the Pegasus

By Josh Coker

Illustrated by Selene Cook

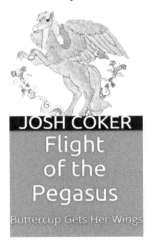

Summary: This is a fairy tale about a pink pony named Buttercup. She wishes she was special like the other animals in the forest. After speaking with the wise owl, Amos, Buttercup sets out on an adventure to find a Unicorn. Little does she know, her world is about to change forever.

About Story Ninjas

Story Ninjas Publishing is an independent book publisher. Our stories range from science fiction to paranormal romance. Our goal is to create stories that are not only entertaining, but endearing. We believe engaging narrative can lead to personal growth. Through unforgettable characters and powerful plot we portray themes that are relevant for today's issues.

You can find more Story Ninja's products here.

Follow Story Ninjas!!!
Twitter: @StoryNinjas
Youtube: @StoryNinjas
Amazon: Story Ninjas
G+: +Story Ninjas
Facebook: StoryNinjasHQ
LinkedIn: Story-Ninjas
Blogger: Story-NinjasHQ

About The Author

Josh is a military veteran and father of three. Many of his children books are based on bedtime stories he told his kids when they were younger. Josh also writes science fiction and creative nonfiction. In 2014 he published a book on military transitions called *About Face.*

You can learn more about Josh by checking out his youtube channel, or his website. Feel free to follow Josh on social media, to find to get updates on all of his latest projects:

Instagram: @Joshumusprime
Facebook: Josh Coker
YouTube: @Tipperdy
Twitter: @Joshumusprime
LinkedIn: Joshua Coker
Amazon: Josh-Coker

CPSIA information can be obtained
at www.ICGtesting.com
Printed in the USA
LVHW082258070120
642877LV00017B/1119/P

9 781546 861256